The Silly Sneeze

ISBN: 1500997900
ISBN 13:9781500997908

Written By: Kathy Berg and Barbara Berg Mies
Illustrations By: Megan Larouere

A strange thing happened to Mr. Sillie one day
A butterfly tickled him and fluttered away

It tickled his nose and tickled his knees
Tickling his nose made Mr. Sillie sneeze

There had never been a sneeze quite like this before
The most humungous, gigantic, explosion galore!

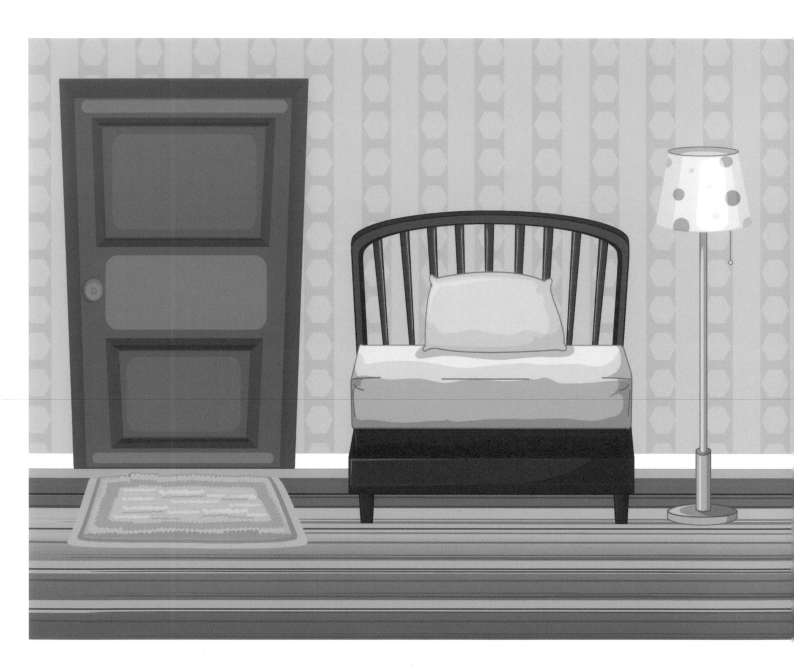

Mr. Sillie felt like something didnt feel right
He looked in the mirror and laughed at the sight

He had sneezed so hard his nose wasnt there
He found it under the table, right under the chair

He tried to pick it up and stubbed his toe
Mr. Sillie's big toe fell off, just like his nose

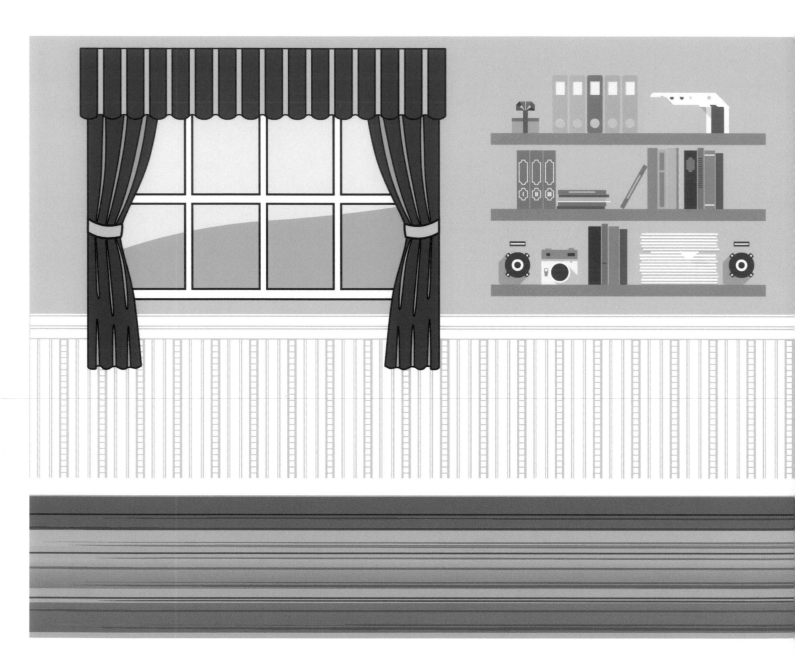

He smiled and laughed and put them back in place
But he put his nose on his foot and his toe on his face!

Oh what a silly day it turned out to be
When he put his toe where his nose should be

What would happen every time he had to sneeze or cough?
Mr. Sillie's socks and shoes would fly off!

Mr. Sillie couldnt stay like this, he began to worry
He came up with a plan, but he needed to hurry

Before this big problem could get any worse
He needed to sneeze again, as big as the first

Mr. Sillie remembered and ran to the tree
He looked for that butterfly, oh where could it be!

He spotted that butterfly way up in the sky
Well that wouldnt work, Mr. Sillie can't fly

Mr. Sillie wasn't looking and bumped into the tree
His nose fell off his foot and his toe fell on his knee.

He picked them both up and didn't bother to see
That he put them in place, just where they should be.

Mr. Sillie felt fine and put back into place
With his toe on his foot and his nose on his face.

Now everything is fine, Mr. Sillie is okay
And that was the end of Mr. Sillie's silly day.

The Silly Sneeze

The Silly Sneeze

CPSIA information can be obtained at www.ICGtesting.com
Printed in the USA
LVIW01n0219260315
432088LV00006B/40